THE LIVING GOSPEL

Daily Devotions for Lent 2020

Greg Kandra

AVE MARIA PRESS AVE Notre Dame, Indiana

Founded in 1865, Ave Maria Press is a ministry of the United States Province of Holy Cross.

www.avemariapress.com

Paperback: ISBN-13 978-1-59471-910-3

E-book: ISBN-13 978-1-59471-911-0

Cover image "At the Foot of the Cross" © Jeni Butler, artworkbyjeni.wix.com.

Cover and text design by John R. Carson.

Printed and bound in the United States of America.

INTRODUCTION

Some years back, the writer Mary Karr published a beautiful memoir of her life and her conversion to Catholicism. Some have actually compared it to the *Confessions* of St. Augustine. Karr's book is called *Lit*. The title refers not only to literature but also to the idea of carrying within you a kind of light, of being "lit."

It's not always easy reading. Karr writes about growing up in an abusive, alcoholic home; about her early, unsatisfying marriage; and about her own struggles with addiction and time she spent in a mental hospital.

At one point, she describes her father's final illness. The family knew he was deteriorating, and they brought him home to die. He often had difficulty speaking. But repeatedly, surprisingly, he managed to communicate one simple word: "Garfield." Well, he had an orange Garfield-the-cat coffee mug by his bed, and people thought he was talking about that.

But his daughter Mary realized, after a time, the real meaning and poignancy of that one word: "Garfield." He wasn't talking about a cartoon cat. He never even read the comic page in the paper. No, Mary realized that word meant something else. It was the family's address: 4901 Garfield Street. He was talking about where he lived. "Garfield," to him, meant home. Safety. Security. Even, perhaps, love. He wanted everyone to know that was where he was, where he wanted to be, and where he belonged.

And so it is, I think, with all of us. It's one reason we observe Lent, why we head to church to get ashes, why we go without meat or chocolate or television and slip an extra folded bill into the collection basket on Sunday or volunteer at a soup kitchen on Thursday. We need to make things right. We want to return to God. We want to be home.

It turns out that's what God wants too. "Return to me, with your whole heart," we hear at the beginning of the season, on Ash Wednesday. We are prodigal children, who have drifted away. We need to be back where we belong, in the arms of a loving father. And so we begin the return: Lent, the long forty-day walk back.

Lent is a penitential season, a time for doing without. Ashes are just the beginning. Our music becomes simpler, our liturgies plainer. The "Gloria" is gone from Sunday Mass. We fast, we pray. We may give up chocolates or meat or television. But for all of this season's sobriety, we shouldn't lose sight of something vitally important: this is a journey we undertake with joy.

Part of that is because we are seeking to draw closer to God, the source and summit of our happiness. But part of it, I think, is something else too, something that goes to our roots as Catholic Christians.

It's right there, in our baptism. When we were baptized, our parents and godparents received a tiny flame, a burning candle, with the words, "Receive the light of Christ." Well, that light still burns. Maybe it's dimmed. Maybe it is only a small ember now. Maybe it's had to struggle against wind and cold. Maybe we've ignored it, or forgotten it. But the light is there.

So yes, this season begins with ashes.

But Lent? Lent is about the fire.

Over these forty days, it's good to ask ourselves, how can we fan the flame and make it grow? How can we turn a flicker into a blaze? Or to invoke the title of Mary Karr's memoir, how can we show the world that we are *lit*?

On Ash Wednesday, ashes—the remnant of a flame—are placed on our brows. And the great work of these Lenten days begins. The work of conversion and repentance. The work of praying more faithfully, loving more deeply. At the beginning, all we see are ashes. But Lent is about something more: working to fan the flame, rediscovering something we may have too easily forgotten, and allowing the light of Christ to show us the way of returning home to the arms of our loving God.

In spite of sin and indifference, in spite of living in a world crowded by cynicism and doubt, we are still what our baptism proclaimed us to be. We are "children of the light." And the candle still burns.

February 26
Ash Wednesday

BEGIN

Lord, open my lips and my mouth shall proclaim your praise.

PRAY

> A clean heart create for me, O God, and a steadfast spirit renew within me.
>
> ~*Psalm 51:12–13*

LISTEN

> *Read Matthew 6:1–6, 16–18.*
>
> "When you pray, go to your inner room, close the door, and pray to your Father in secret. And your Father who sees in secret will repay you."

Works in Progress

When I was in high school, I had an English teacher by the name of Mrs. Comberiatti. One day she came into class wearing a big button on her lapel. More than forty years later, I don't remember much of what she taught us about *The Scarlett Letter* or *A Tale of Two Cities*. But I do remember that button. It said, "Please be patient. God isn't finished with me yet." Whether we realize it or not, today we proclaim that same message. We will proclaim it not with a button on a lapel . . . but with ashes on our foreheads.

The ashes we wear announce to the world this plain fact: we are sinners. They tell all who see us that we are beginning this season of prayer, repentance, and sacrifice—that we are seeking to reconcile ourselves with

God. These ashes announce that we are works in progress. They say, "Please be patient. God isn't finished with me yet." He isn't finished with any of us. That is the great wonder and consolation of Lent.

As we enter this holy season, we should approach it with seriousness. But we shouldn't mistake that seriousness for solemnity. The gospel today reminds us, "Do not look gloomy . . . anoint your head and wash your face." I'd take that one step further: add to this season a sense of possibility. Make it an occasion for hope. A new start. It begins here, and now.

As we "remember that you are dust, and to dust you will return," let's remember, too, to be patient—with ourselves. And with everyone else. Because God isn't finished with any of us yet.

ACT

Today, I will remind myself that I am a work in progress. God isn't finished with me yet. How can I make God's work easier and become more patient, more understanding, and more loving?

PRAY

Be merciful, O Lord, for I have sinned. Help me to spend these days ahead repairing what is broken, and healing what is wounded, so that I will grow in love for you and those around me.

February 27

Thursday after Ash Wednesday

BEGIN

Lord, open my lips and my mouth shall proclaim your praise.

PRAY

> Blessed is the man who does not walk in the counsel of the wicked, nor stand in the way of sinners. Amen.
>
> ~*Psalm 1:1*

LISTEN

> *Read Luke 9:22–25.*
>
> "What profit is there to gain the whole world yet lose or forfeit himself?"

Cross-Training

In 2018, Nike caused a sensation with an ad using the tagline, "Believe in something. Even if it means sacrificing everything. Just do it." If it sounds familiar, it should. In some ways it echoes what Jesus says in today's gospel: "Take up your cross and follow me." But Jesus, of course, offers his disciples something that Nike can't: salvation. "Whoever loses his life for my sake and that of the Gospel will save it." In other words, believe in something, even if it means sacrificing everything. It is a powerful message for an ad, and for all of us, especially during Lent.

But the Christian message is not just to believe in *something*; rather, it is about believing in *someone*. That someone, of course, is Jesus. Believe in him—not just that he exists but also that he is the way to salvation.

And then, prepare to sacrifice everything. Because this is what it means to be Christian.

Being Christian means loving your neighbor and praying for your persecutors. It means prayer and fasting. It means turning the other cheek, giving away your cloak, and bending to bandage the broken, bleeding man by the side of the road. It means feeding the hungry and clothing the naked—and doing it because this is what we believe, because this is what was passed on to us by God's own son.

This isn't always easy. Sometimes, the cross becomes too heavy. The sacrifices we need to make, especially during Lent, can be daunting. But Christ reminds us that the sacrifice and hardship are worth it—and that love comes at a cost. The cost, he assures us though, is worth it. Make the choice, he says. Believe—and then begin. Just do it.

ACT

This day, I will not look for the easy way out. What are the daily crosses I avoid carrying? I will seek opportunities to help others carry their crosses and ease their burden.

PRAY

Be merciful, O Lord, for I have sinned. How often have I sought things for my own personal benefit and ignored the needs of others? Help me, Lord, to draw closer to you. Amen.

FEBRUARY 28

FRIDAY AFTER ASH WEDNESDAY

BEGIN

Lord, open my lips and my mouth shall proclaim your praise.

PRAY

> Have mercy on me, O God, in your goodness; in the greatness of your compassion wipe out my offense.
>
> ~*Psalm 51:3–4*

LISTEN

Read Matthew 9:14–15.

"The day will come when the bridegroom is taken away."

Fasting from Indifference

The gospel today mentions a critical part of our Lenten practice, and one we need to take to heart: fasting. But do we completely grasp what we are undertaking?

Fridays during Lent, of course, are traditionally days of fasting or abstinence; we go without a meal or abstain from meat and reflect more deeply on Christ's ultimate sacrifice, what he gave for us on the Cross. So yes, we typically think of Lent as a time for giving up, but I always like to remind people, "Remember, 'giving up' begins with 'giving.'" Skipping a meal or forgoing that ham sandwich at lunch may seem noble and spark pangs of hunger. But that's only the beginning. Is there more we should be doing?

Besides giving up, what are we *giving*? Are we giving to the poor? Are we increasing donations to Catholic

Charities or programs that feed the hungry? Are we giving of ourselves more? Are we checking in with lonely neighbors, visiting the sick, or volunteering our time and talents to those in need? Are we giving more time to consider those who go without every day, not just during Lent? Those who are poor, homeless, or hungry?

As we spend idle moments this season hungering for what we've given up, do we think of those who always hunger, and not only for physical food? Do we consider the needs of those who hunger for dignity, friendship, or self-worth? Do we consider those who hunger for love?

While we fast from relatively easy things such as food, let us pray this season for the grace to fast from the harder things such as selfishness, apathy, pettiness, and inflated egos.

Lent is a time for giving up. And it's also a wonderful opportunity to become better at the art of giving.

ACT

What are the things I have a difficult time giving up (besides chocolate or radio on the way to work)? Just for today, I will work to give up those things that are keeping me from drawing closer to God—and pray for perseverance in giving more to others in small but meaningful ways.

PRAY

Be merciful, O Lord, for I have sinned. Help me to give up temptations to sin and learn how to give in a spirit of sacrifice and love. Amen.

FEBRUARY 29

SATURDAY AFTER ASH WEDNESDAY

BEGIN

Lord, open my lips and my mouth shall proclaim your praise.

PRAY

Teach me your way, O LORD, that I may walk in your truth.

~Psalm 86:1

LISTEN

Read Luke 5:27–32.

"I have not come to call the righteous to repentance but sinners."

Following Jesus

Did he have any idea what he was getting himself into? Sitting there, counting his money, did the man known as Levi realize what it would mean to respond when Jesus said, "Follow me"? Did he know that when he got up and followed he was beginning the most challenging journey of his life, one that would take him to mountains and miracles, to Gethsemane and Golgotha? How could he have known? None of them did. But they followed, and with one lone exception, they stayed, all the way to the end.

Some years back, *ABC News* attempted to unravel the mystery of Christianity and get to the bottom of "the real Jesus." Peter Jennings interviewed historians and theologians in an effort to determine what actually happened in Galilee all those centuries ago. Could the life and death of this man called Jesus have been some sort of fabrication? Was it little more than a cult? What he found may have surprised a few people: the experts concluded that *something* had happened. *Something* had compelled people to answer the call of Jesus to follow and to continue following him, even after his death and resurrection. They were at a loss to explain it. Resurrection? Maybe. But *something* defying rational explanation turned doubters into believers and followers into martyrs and saints.

We who believe call that "something" faith—faith that compels us to rise from our ordinary, sinful, muddled lives and follow Jesus. During these weeks of Lent, we encounter him once again gazing at us, inviting us, and beckoning us: "Follow me." How courageous will we be? How far will we go with him and for him?

ACT

I have not always followed Jesus as closely or as faithfully as I should. Today, that changes. Today, when he calls me, I will answer yes. I will leave behind the things that hold me down and rise to follow him.

PRAY

Be merciful, O Lord, for I have sinned. I rise today to follow you and trust that you will lead me, encourage me, support me, and walk with me wherever you need me to go on my Lenten journey. Amen.

Sunday, March 1
First Week of Lent

BEGIN

Lord, open my lips and my mouth shall proclaim your praise.

PRAY

> Blessed is the one whose fault is removed, whose sin is forgiven.
>
> *~Psalm 32:1*

LISTEN

> *Read Matthew 4:1–11.*
>
> Then Jesus was led by the Spirit into the desert to be tempted by the devil.

What We Give Up

If we think these forty days are hard on us, look at what Jesus did for forty days and how God's Word, intense prayer, and sheer willpower can conquer temptation. This gospel reading reminds us that Christ had to struggle with very human needs and desires. He understands what we are going through—not just during Lent but always.

But what exactly *are* we going through? What temptations are we fighting? Not long ago, Google decided to find out. The search engine looked at online searches containing the terms "Lent" and "give up." It then broke down the results state by state. The most popular item, in eight of fifty states, was meat. Alcohol came in second, in seven states. Six states were giving up sweets or sugar. The list, of course, is hardly exhaustive.

As we begin our journey into Lent, we might want to ask ourselves what other temptations are calling out to us that more directly keep us from following the way of Christ more fully. Are we being tempted to condemn others too easily? Do we feel dark joy when others stumble, fall, or fail? Do we too easily believe the worst about others, instead of looking for the best? Are we preoccupied with gossip or snapping at others online? Perhaps these are the things we *really* need to give up.

But know this: whether we're trying to do without chocolate, alcohol, or meat, or an inflated ego, pettiness, gossip, or judging others, the sacrifice is well worth it. Because what we give up during this season is nothing compared to what we can receive if we open ourselves to God's saving grace.

ACT

Today, I will seek the best in others. I will resist judging their weaknesses and find ways to appreciate and affirm to them their strengths.

PRAY

Be merciful, O Lord, for I have sinned. Give me a spirit that helps me give up those things that are keeping me from you, and help me grow in generosity. Amen.

MONDAY, MARCH 2
FIRST WEEK OF LENT

BEGIN

Lord, open my lips and my mouth shall proclaim your praise.

PRAY

"Be holy, for I, the LORD your God, am holy."

~*Leviticus 19:1–2*

LISTEN

Read Matthew 25:31–46.

"Whatever you did for one of these least brothers of mine, you did for me."

Christ's Favorite Virtue

Before he became the cardinal archbishop of New York, Timothy Dolan was the rector of the North American College in Rome. He used to give regular talks to the seminarians, which were collected in a book called *Priests for the Third Millennium*. In one of the talks, Cardinal Dolan quotes a retreat conference given by the Passionist scripture scholar Barnabas Ahern.

Fr. Ahern asked, "What do you suppose was Jesus Christ's favorite virtue? Was it faith? Was it hope? How about charity or justice?" All of those are contenders. But Fr. Ahern had something else in mind. Christ's favorite virtue, he suggested, was humility, and he made a persuasive argument.

Again and again in the gospels, Christ chose the most humble and preached compassion for the smallest, the weakest, and the sickest. The gospels offer a reassuring message for all of us who feel unworthy, or fall short; they offer this blessed hope: Jesus often found *more* among those who, in the eyes of the world, seemed to be *less*.

Today's gospel passage, Matthew 25, calls on us to do the same: to seek out those whom others ignore, to help those who are shunned, and to lift up those who are put down. In doing so, we ourselves can exercise humility, that most favorite virtue, and find kinship with others.

Lent is a chance for us to acknowledge and embrace humility. We began this season with ashes on our brows, to show our mortality. What else can we do to show our compassion for others? What can we do to show solidarity with all who suffer?

Jesus reminds us that this is one of the greatest things we can do, because in caring for them, we care for him.

ACT

Today, I will look for Jesus in all those I encounter, in every situation, and look on them with love.

PRAY

Be merciful, O Lord, for I have sinned. Help me to see you in all people and love them as I love you. Amen.

TUESDAY, MARCH 3
FIRST WEEK OF LENT

BEGIN

Lord, open my lips and my mouth shall proclaim your praise.

PRAY

> I sought the LORD and he answered me and delivered me from all my fears.
>
> ~Psalm 34:6–7

LISTEN

Read Matthew 6:7–15.

"When you pray, go to your inner room, close the door, and pray to your Father in secret."

Inner Sanctum

Dr. Andrew Newburg, of Philadelphia's Thomas Jefferson Hospital, has studied the positive impact of prayer on the human body. He told *NBC News* several years ago that prayer has a distinct and mysterious ability to change us: "You become connected to God. You become connected to the world. Your self sort of goes away."

Isn't that what we try to achieve during Lent? This is a time for seeking to be more "connected to God," giving ourselves more to him and to others. It is a season for renewal, recommitment, and returning to God with our hearts. What Newburg described suggests just why prayer is a cornerstone of our Lenten practices, and in today's gospel reading, Jesus offers his followers—and us—the definitive prescription for prayer. It is probably the best-known prayer in the world, one whose first two words sum up so much of what connects us to God: "Our Father."

But Jesus does more than just give us the words to say; he also gives us the way to say them, privately, in our "inner room . . . in secret." The deepest expression of our devotion to God needs to happen in solitude, where we speak and God listens—and where he speaks and *we* listen.

At this early moment in the Lenten season, this scripture speaks of the power of prayer to bring about intimacy with God, a new sense of belonging to him and even, as Newburg suggested, a way to be changed. In our broken human condition, if we truly want to be healed, prayer may be just what the doctor ordered.

ACT

I will try today to pray as simply and honestly as I can. I will find a quiet corner, my "inner room," and open my heart to God just for a few moments. What will he say to me? I will be listening.

PRAY

Be merciful, O Lord, for I have sinned. Guide my thoughts, words, and deeds to bring me home to you, where I long to be. Amen.

WEDNESDAY, MARCH 4
FIRST WEEK OF LENT

BEGIN

Lord, open my lips and my mouth shall proclaim your praise.

PRAY

A heart contrite and humbled, O God, you will not spurn.

~*Psalm 51*

LISTEN

Read Luke 11:29–32.

"This generation is an evil generation; it seeks a sign, but no sign will be given it, except the sign of Jonah."

Repent!

Reminding his listeners about the story of Jonah, Jesus was summoning memories of a great prophet who was sent to warn the people of Nineveh. Along the way, Jonah encountered a storm at sea and ended up spending three days in the belly of a giant fish (in popular lore, a whale). Only after he survived did people listen, believe, and repent. But this is more than just a fish story. By comparing himself to Jonah, Jesus was foreshadowing his own three days in the tomb. Yet he was doing more than following in the footsteps of that prophet; he was also continuing the message of John the Baptist with a clarion call to repent. It may not have been a message a lot of his listeners wanted to hear. Do we?

During these first days of Lent, this passage can give us a jolt: "This generation is an evil generation." But maybe that's what we need to hear. Maybe right about now we need to be pulled back to the sackcloth-and-ashes attitude of last week's Ash Wednesday. Maybe now we need to remember what it's all about.

Let's take these words of Jesus as words of warning—but also words of hope. We can be more than what we have been. Let's make the sign of Jonah that sign we saw in the mirror on Ash Wednesday, the ashes that mark us as mortal and remind us, whether we want to hear it or not, that we will one day be dust.

What will we do about it? And what will we do with the time we have now?

ACT

Jesus, like John the Baptist before him, is calling on his followers to repent. This day, I will do a fearless moral inventory and ask myself again, What do I want to change about myself during the rest of Lent? How have I fallen short? How can I be more than I am?

PRAY

Be merciful, O Lord, for I have sinned. Help me recognize what I need to change, and give me the courage and help me trust in your mercy to become the person you want me to be.

Thursday, March 5
First Week of Lent

BEGIN

Lord, open my lips and my mouth shall proclaim your praise.

PRAY

Lord, on the day I called for help, you answered me.

~Psalm 138:1

LISTEN

Read Matthew 7:7–12.

"Ask and it will be given to you; seek and you will find."

Ask, Seek, Knock, Trust

A popular method of team-building is the "trust exercise," in which members of a team, standing in a circle and surrounded by others, close their eyes and just fall back into the empty air, trusting that people will catch them. If you're skeptical or generally leery of trust, it can be terrifying. Will the hands and arms be there? Or will you land with a thud?

Prayer is like that too. It may be one reason we do it so infrequently and so poorly; we just don't trust that God will be there, or that he is even listening. But in this gospel passage, Jesus reassures us. "Trust," he says. "Have faith. Seek. Knock. God will not abandon you. He will give you what you need. More importantly, he will give you what you seek." But what is that? I think that the seeking—the search—goes deeper, and further, than we usually comprehend.

When a father prays for his sick child to get well, when a woman prays for her husband to find a job, or when we as a people pray for peace, what are we truly seeking? It may be something we can barely name. Maybe it's life. Or hope. Or freedom from fear. It may simply be to realize that we are loved.

In many ways, our experience of Lent is, in part, a trust exercise, throwing ourselves into God's arms with faith, with love, and yes, with trust. During Lent, we profess our childlike trust in God's goodness and mercy. Are we willing to "let go and let God"?

Loving arms will be there, no matter what. Don't be afraid. God will catch us if we fall.

ACT

Today, I will share with God my hopes and fears. I will bring my deepest anxieties to him in prayer and trust that he will hold me in his loving arms.

PRAY

Be merciful, O Lord, for I have sinned. To you I come, seeking, asking, and knocking, certain that you will know what I seek and help me to discover it. Amen.

FRIDAY, MARCH 6
FIRST WEEK OF LENT

Lord, open my lips and my mouth shall proclaim your praise.

> My soul waits for the Lord more than sentinels wait
> for the dawn.
>
> *~Psalm 130:6*

Read Matthew 5:20–26.

"Go first and be reconciled with your brother."

Reconciliation

One of my favorite places to go to Confession in Manhattan is St. Francis of Assisi on Thirty-Second Street, near Pennsylvania Station. They have Franciscan friars hearing Confession all day long. The friars are popular too; there's almost always a line. Personally, I like them because they aren't scary. Many years ago, after I'd been away from the sacrament for several years, I went there for Confession, and when I told the friar how long it had been since my last Confession, he said very gently, and very simply, "Welcome back." Those were the most beautiful words I'd ever heard—not only words of welcome but also words that held out the promise of healing and reconciliation.

The gospel reading this Friday in Lent is all about being reconciled with those around us, but I think it also offers us a key to reconciling with God. Don't put off mending fences, Jesus says. Make peace with someone you've drifted away from. Heal divisions. Begin anew.

Friday, a day of abstinence from meat during this season, is a good day to remember that we should often fast from more than just meat. How about fasting from fear, mistrust, or laziness in our prayer life? It can also be a good time to drop by a church to celebrate the Sacrament of Reconciliation.

"Be reconciled with your brother," Jesus told his disciples. This is a good time to ask ourselves, Do we also need to reconcile with the Father?

ACT

Is there someone in my life I've neglected or harmed? Today, I will work to reconcile with that someone—whether it's a friend, a family member, a coworker, or a neighbor—or perhaps it is God.

PRAY

Be merciful, O Lord, for I have sinned. I'm sorry for all I've done that has hurt others or hurt you. Give me the grace to begin again as a better person. Amen.

Saturday, March 7
First Week of Lent

BEGIN

Lord, open my lips and my mouth shall proclaim your praise.

PRAY

> Blessed are they who follow the law of the Lord.
>
> *~Psalm 119:1*

LISTEN

Read Matthew 5:43–48.

"Love your enemies, and pray for those who persecute you."

The Impossible Command

Years ago, when I delivered my very first homily on an Ash Wednesday, I offered a modest proposal. "Try something truly challenging this Lent," I said. "Try praying for people you don't like. Maybe, even, try praying for people you hate or who hate you. Pray for an enemy." Then I had an idea.

"Consider this," I said. "When was the last time anyone in this church prayed for Osama bin Laden?" As if on cue, hundreds of people gasped. After Mass, several people told me I was asking too much. They didn't think they could do that. Well, I explained, it wasn't my idea. Jesus came up with it first.

And here it is: "Love your enemies and pray for those who persecute you." Honestly, this may be one of the hardest commands in all of scripture, and it challenges us in ways we think are impossible. So how do we begin?

Writer Emmett Fox, in his book *Sermon on the Mount*, explains it in a way I think we all can understand. And it starts with something so simple, but so hard: forgiveness. It is a necessary first step. He says that by not forgiving we are "tied to the thing [we] hate. The person perhaps in the whole world whom you most dislike is the very one to whom you are attaching yourself by a hook that is stronger than steel. Is this what you wish?"

This Lent, let's get ourselves off the hook. Take that first step. Forgive. Then love. Then pray. What would Jesus do? I think we know the answer.

ACT

Who is my enemy? Who is my persecutor? This day, I will whisper a prayer for him or her, and begin in some small way to love someone I would rather keep hating.

PRAY

Be merciful, O Lord, for I have sinned. Teach me to love as you loved, to forgive as you forgave, and to pray as you prayed—not only for those I care about but also for those I don't.

Sunday, March 8
Second Week of Lent

BEGIN

Lord, open my lips and my mouth shall proclaim your praise.

PRAY

> My help comes from the LORD, the maker of heaven and earth.
>
> *~Psalm 121:2*

LISTEN

Read Matthew 17:1–9.

"Lord, it is good for us to be here."

Rise and Do Not Be Afraid

How is your Lent going? Right about now, just eleven days in, is when the fervor starts to wear off. The things we gave up—chocolate, television, social media, and desserts—are tugging at us, distracting us again, and looking better and better.

That's not uncommon, and I think it's part of what makes us human, what makes our Lenten journey so challenging—and so vital. And it is, first and foremost, a journey. I'm reminded of Sr. Teresa Benedicta of the Cross, better known as Edith Stein, a brilliant German Jewish woman who was baptized Catholic in 1922. Just twenty years later, she lost her life at Auschwitz. Today, she is recognized as a saint.

Stein once spoke of what it takes to be a Christian. "Whoever belongs to Christ," she said, "must go the whole way with him. He must mature to adulthood.

He must one day or other walk the way of the cross to Gethsemane and Golgotha." We realize why in today's gospel, when we follow another journey—up a mountain—where Jesus is miraculously transfigured. The apostles are so terrified; they can't even look. But Jesus comforts them. "Rise," he says, "and do not be afraid."

And so he speaks to us, wherever we are on our journey. "Rise, and do not be afraid." Take heart. Yes, there will be setbacks and stumbles. We will make mistakes. But that, too, is part of our journey. Remember why we are following this path, making these sacrifices, and trying to turn our hearts back to God. We strive toward a paradise we can't begin to imagine, where Christ dwells in light and in love.

He is waiting for us, hoping for us, and praying for us. So rise. And don't be afraid!

ACT

I will be patient with myself today and with others I meet, remembering that we are all on a journey. Every one of us encounters stumbles, setbacks, and challenges.

PRAY

Be merciful, O Lord, for I have sinned. Help me to be merciful to others, as you are merciful to me. Amen.

Monday, March 9

Second Week of Lent

BEGIN

Lord, open my lips and my mouth shall proclaim your praise.

PRAY

> Remember not against us the iniquities of the past;
> may your compassion quickly come to us.

~*Psalm 79:8*

LISTEN

Read Luke 6:36–38.

"Be merciful as your Father is merciful."

Share This

These days, to dwell in the world of social media—Facebook, Twitter, Instagram, or Snapchat—means we are constantly passing judgment. We like. We share. We dislike. We condemn. We comment. We laugh. We approve. And for *what*? We end up weighing in on everything from the hottest movies to the president's statements. Everybody has an opinion (or thinks they have to). And we often wonder whether every opinion is equally valid and worthy of attention. The result leads to noise, *lots* of noise, and some of the liveliest (and often nastiest) exchanges. It can also draw us as Christians further from Christ.

Small wonder, then, that in today's gospel reading, Jesus says, in effect, "Knock it off." His message is clear and direct. Don't judge; instead, be merciful. Give to others. Forgive. Is it really that hard for us to grasp?

Well, yes. These things go against our human nature. We want to judge, and of course we like to feel superior to those we're judging. But Christ's teaching tells us we need to convert our hearts, our thoughts, and our actions. We need to be better. And isn't that central to our observance of Lent?

This short passage sums up so much of what we all need to work on, pray on, and pray about during our Lenten journey. To paraphrase John the Baptist, we need to decrease so Christ can increase. Still wondering what to give up for Lent? Consider giving up judgment in favor of prayer and mercy. In a world consumed with sharing nearly everything on social media, that's one choice we all should be sharing.

ACT

Too often, we feel compelled to offer our judgments and opinions. Just for today, I will hold back. I will strive to be a person of mercy and forgiveness, a true follower of Jesus.

PRAY

Be merciful, O Lord, for I have sinned. Teach me to be as merciful as you are, and to give to others with generosity of spirit, from a spirit of love. Amen.

Tuesday, March 10
Second Week of Lent

BEGIN

Lord, open my lips and my mouth shall proclaim your praise.

PRAY

> Wash yourselves clean! Put away your misdeeds
> from before my eyes; cease doing evil; learn to do
> good. Make justice your aim: redress the wronged;
> hear the orphan's plea, defend the widow.
>
> ~Isaiah 1:16–17

LISTEN

Read Matthew 23:1–12.

"The greatest among you must be your servant."

Giving Ourselves

A few years ago, I read the remarkable story of Fr. Rick Frechette, an American priest serving the poorest of the poor in Haiti. Ordained a Passionist priest in 1979, he felt called to do something more. He went to Honduras, where he established an orphanage. He later visited Haiti, where he met Mother Teresa's Missionaries of Charity, which had established a home for babies and their critically ill mothers, many of them dying of AIDS.

In Haiti, Fr. Rick started an orphanage called Nos Petits Frères et Soeurs, "Our Little Brothers and Sisters." Despite uncontrollable crime and chaos in the country, the orphanage has not only survived but also thrived. At one dangerous point, during an economic embargo, Fr. Rick was urged to leave the country. He refused.

"How could we leave the children?" he asked. "What kind of shepherd would leave when the wolf comes?"

After a few years, Fr. Rick decided to go to medical school. Once licensed as a doctor, he began working at a clinic in Port-au-Prince, a clinic with no water, no electricity, and few medical supplies. He gives everything for those who have nothing, often working with little more than a heart full of love. A friend of mine posted Fr. Rick's story on his blog and concluded, about us Catholic Christians, "It's what our kind do best."

When Jesus tells us, "The greatest among you must be your servant," he had people such as Fr. Rick Frechette in mind.

But what about us? This Lent, how far are we willing to go to sacrifice for others? How much of ourselves are we willing to give up to show the face of Christ to those in need?

ACT

How can I humbly serve others? In what way can I use my time and talent to uplift those in need? Today, in a world where so many want to be served, I will look for opportunities to be a servant.

PRAY

Be merciful, O Lord, for I have sinned. Help me to learn humility and to live it every day. Amen.

WEDNESDAY, MARCH 11
SECOND WEEK OF LENT

BEGIN

Lord, open my lips and my mouth shall proclaim your praise.

PRAY

Into your hands I commend my spirit.

~Psalm 31:6

LISTEN

Read Matthew 20:17–28.

"The Son of Man did not come to be served but to serve and to give his life as a ransom for many."

Serving like Christ

Do you sense a theme this week? In yesterday's gospel reading, Jesus told his followers that the greatest must serve others. Today, he sets himself up as an example for that, explaining that he himself has come to serve. Today's discussion comes in response to the mother of James and John, but when she says she wants her sons to have choice seats in the kingdom, isn't she really speaking for many of us? How often do we look for our own personal gain? How often do we ask ourselves, What's in it for me? How often do we spend our lives planning ways to climb the ladder or scale the heights? We can spend endless hours wondering, or worrying, plotting, and fantasizing. Jesus wants to remind us that our lives are meant for something else, and pointedly, he makes clear that there is no crown without the cross.

As we strive during Lent to turn our thoughts inward, seeking to convert our hearts, we need also to direct our thoughts outward, seeking to help others first. Whoever wishes to be great, Jesus says, must first serve. The ones who wish to scale the heights can't do it on the backs of others—and shouldn't expect a heavenly reward for it. We are called to something else: to lives of sacrifice, of care and commitment, of service and humility.

Imagine what would happen if the most powerful and influential figures in the world worked, above all, as humble slaves to their brothers and sisters. Now, imagine if all of us did that. Not only would that mean acting as true Christians, true followers of Christ, but also it would mean acting like Christ himself.

ACT

Am I humble enough, selfless enough, and compassionate enough? Today, I will try to follow Christ more closely by seeking not to be served but to serve.

PRAY

Be merciful, O Lord, for I have sinned. Help me to have a servant's heart, to be full of a willingness to serve others with humility and joy. Amen.

Thursday March 12
Second Week of Lent

BEGIN

Lord, open my lips and my mouth shall proclaim your praise.

PRAY

> The LORD watches over the way of the just.
>
> ~*Psalm 1:6*

LISTEN

> *Read Luke 16:19–31.*
>
> "Father Abraham, have pity on me!"

Perhaps the Miracle Is You

A few years ago, walking to work in New York, I passed a young woman sitting on the sidewalk holding a cardboard sign. "Praying for a miracle," it said. Next to her was a shoebox filled with a few coins people had dropped in. I was late for work and, like thousands of others on Third Avenue that morning, just kept walking by. But the image of her stayed with me. Later, on my lunch hour, I went to see if she was still there. She was gone, another mysterious ghost of the city, anonymous and forgotten. To this day, I wonder what her story was, and if there was something I could have done. Whatever became of her? Did she ever get her miracle? Should I have done something to help her? It pricks my conscience.

In a similar way, the story of Lazarus and the rich man should make us uneasy and challenge us to ask ourselves if we are taking those around us for granted—or, worse, neglecting the poor and needy among us.

Lent is a time for giving alms to the poor, for turning our attention to those in need whom we too often forget: those who are hungry, desperate and alone, depressed or anxious, neglected, or enslaved by human trafficking or addiction—the outcasts. We are always called to remember that the world is full of anonymous souls who are praying for a miracle. This season of repentance and renewal beckons us to remember our calling, to turn toward those in need, to pray with them and for them, and to reach out in some way to help. Give to a soup kitchen. Donate time at a shelter or food pantry. Give to the poor through a charity close to your heart. Who knows? Perhaps the miracle they're praying for . . . is you.

ACT

Today, I will look for a way to donate to an organization that cares for those in need. With my time and skills, or my money, I will give and try to be the face of Christ to someone in need.

PRAY

Be merciful, O Lord, for I have sinned. Help me to be more merciful, too, toward those in need, and guide my heart in the way of generosity and love. Amen.

Friday March 13
Second Week of Lent

BEGIN

Lord, open my lips and my mouth shall proclaim your praise.

PRAY

> Remember the marvels the Lord has done.
>
> ~Psalm 105:5

LISTEN

> *Read Matthew 21:33–43, 45–46.*
>
> "The kingdom of God will be taken away from you and given to a people that will produce its fruit."

What Kind of Fruit Are We Producing?

This reading, with the parable of the tenants, forces us to think about something most of us would probably prefer not to think about: the judgment of God. What will he do with us? How will he judge us? What will be our fate? It's a sobering reminder of something we likely paid closer attention to at the beginning of this season, our mortality. We will not be alive forever, and at some point our bodies will be little more than dust. How are we using the time we've been given? Maybe it's something we need to hear right about now.

Today's gospel reading compels us to think more deeply about how we are caring for what God has given us—our world, our brothers and sisters, and the teachings of Christ—and how we are (or are not) honoring them. More pointedly, the passage makes us ask ourselves what kind of fruit we are producing.

The days of Lent should be days in which we ask that question of ourselves often. These weeks are a period of prayerful self-examination. It's worth asking ourselves, Are we doing what we can to grow in holiness? Are we spending more time in prayer? Are we fasting from things we enjoy and trying to live more simply, to draw closer to the humble spirit of sacrifice and love contained in the Gospel? Or have we forgotten what this is all about?

This reading could serve as a wake-up call, to recommit to our Lenten practices and turn our hearts and our hopes back to the Lord. Someday, there will be a judgment. How do we want God to judge us?

ACT

Today is a good day to do a Lenten checkup. Just for today, I will prayerfully look at my life during Lent and recommit myself to making the most of these forty days, in a spirit of sacrifice and love.

PRAY

Be merciful, O Lord, for I have sinned. Give me the patience and fortitude to continue to give up pettiness, jealousy, and pride for Lent so that I can grow closer to you.

Saturday, March 14
Second Week of Lent

BEGIN

Lord, open my lips and my mouth shall proclaim your praise.

PRAY

> Bless the LORD, O my soul; and all my being, bless his holy name.
>
> ~Psalm 103:1

LISTEN

> Read Luke 15:1–3, 11–32.

> "He was lost and has been found."

The Prodigal, a President, a Pardon

In 1864, a teenager named Roswell McIntyre was drafted into the New York Cavalry during the Civil War. He ended up being sent into battle with very little training. He was terrified, and his fear got the best of him. He ended up running away from his battalion. Not long after, he was caught and tried for desertion. At his court-martial he was found guilty, and for his crime young Roswell McIntyre was sentenced to death by firing squad. Roswell's mother appealed to President Lincoln and pleaded to give her son a second chance. Lincoln's generals told him that pardoning the boy would be devastating for morale and set a bad example. But the president came to another conclusion.

"I have observed," he said, "that it never does a boy much good to shoot him."

He pardoned Roswell, who went on to die in battle, giving his life in service to his country.

Lincoln understood mercy. When someone later asked Lincoln how he planned to treat Southerners who had broken away from the country, the president replied, "I will treat them as if they had never been away." He could have been speaking as the father of the prodigal son.

This parable poses a beautiful lesson about humility and the search for forgiveness. But it also challenges us. Could we forgive as that father did?

How many of us can be that merciful? That means running to meet those who are wounded and who want to come home, and opening your arms to those who want to start over. It means knowing the value of a second chance. It means sparing the Roswell McIntyres who happen to cross your path in life.

Lent is our moment to do that, to believe in redemption, conversion, and hope.

ACT

Is there someone in my life I've been unable to forgive? Today, I will strive to forgive another as the father of the prodigal son forgives—as God, I pray, forgives me.

PRAY

Be merciful, O Lord, for I have sinned. Forgive me, Father, and show me the way to forgive others.

SUNDAY, MARCH 15
THIRD WEEK OF LENT

BEGIN

Lord, open my lips and my mouth shall proclaim your praise.

PRAY

> Come, let us sing joyfully to the LORD; cry out to the rock of our salvation.

> ~Psalm 95:1

LISTEN

Read John 4:5–42.

"We know that this is truly the savior of the world."

Brief Encounter

What would happen if we met Jesus in the middle of an ordinary day? How would we react? Consider the story Satoko Kitahara.

Satoko was a wealthy young woman who lived in Tokyo after World War II. Tokyo was then a city in ruins. The poorest people lived near the river in a place known as "Ant Town," because the poor were considered as insignificant as insects.

In 1949, while walking through the city, Satoko decided out of curiosity to follow a group of nuns into a Catholic church and was quickly transfixed by what she saw. Something touched her deeply. She kept going back to the church. Several months later, at the age of twenty, Satoko—a Shinto Buddhist—asked to be baptized. Not long after, a missionary took her to Ant Town, and Satoko was stunned. She felt called to live among the poor, explaining, "To save us, God sent his only Son to be one of us. It hit me that there was only one way to help these rag-picker children. And it was to become a rag picker like them."

She worked among the people there until she died of tuberculosis at the age of twenty-eight. Many now pray that Satoko Kitahara will one day become a saint.

On this particular Sunday, I think her story echoes the one in our gospel reading, about another woman who met Jesus and was also transformed. The passage reminds us that an encounter with Christ can change everything.

As we continue our Lenten journey, may we be open to encountering Jesus—and being forever changed.

ACT

Today, I will seek Christ in unexpected people and unexpected places, especially the poor and the outcast, on the margins. I will look for concrete ways to open my heart to those in need, by volunteering or giving to the poor.

PRAY

Be merciful, O Lord, for I have sinned. Too often I do not treat others as you want me to treat them. Help soften my heart and open my eyes to your presence in others.

MONDAY, MARCH 16
THIRD WEEK OF LENT

BEGIN

Lord, open my lips and my mouth shall proclaim your praise.

PRAY

> As the hind longs for running waters, so my soul longs for you, O God.

> ~*Psalm 42:2*

LISTEN

> *Read Luke 4:24–30.*

> "Amen, I say to you, no prophet is accepted in his own native place."

The Out-of-Towners

Anyone who works in a parish Rite of Christian Initiation of Adults (RCIA) program will tell you, often the most fervent and devoted members of the parish are the converts. They are the lectors and extraordinary ministers of Holy Communion who always show up, the ones who most consistently arrive early for Mass and stay after to pray; they get involved in everything from being ushers to working on the stewardship committee. The conversion experience, or being received into full communion with the Church, leaves a lasting mark. Indeed, some of the towering figures of our faith in the modern era have been people such as Edith Stein, Avery Dulles, and Evelyn Waugh, people who embraced the faith after years as atheists or agnostics.

I've found from my own experience that being a cradle believer means we might sometimes take the faith for granted, which seems to be exactly the problem Christ encounters in this gospel. People in his "native place," Nazareth, have a hard time accepting what he has to say. He reminds us that those outside the circle are sometimes more receptive to God's Word.

Right now, there are some of us, I'm sure, who feel outside the circle, somehow apart from God. But these are the ones who need his message, and the message of Lent, most! Lent calls us to reconnect, as children of God, as Christians, and as people longing (like the deer in the psalm) to be nourished by the Lord.

ACT

This day, I will remember that God's message was meant for everyone. What does he want me to hear? What does he want me to do?

PRAY

Be merciful, O Lord, for I have sinned. I know I have cut myself off from you. But I also know you hold open the door for my return. Welcome me back, and help me to discover the way home. Amen.

TUESDAY, MARCH 17
THIRD WEEK OF LENT

BEGIN

Lord, open my lips and my mouth shall proclaim your praise.

PRAY

Remember your mercies, O LORD.

~Psalm 25:6

LISTEN

Read Matthew 18:21–35.

"Lord, if my brother sins against me, how often must I forgive him?"

"How Great Is This Forgiveness!"

In April 2017, the world was horrified by terror attacks that left dozens dead in Coptic churches in Egypt. But two weeks after the attacks, we saw, unexpectedly, a beautiful witness to the faith—and a testament to the very subject at the heart of today's gospel reading, forgiveness.

It happened on Egyptian television. A reporter interviewed the widow of Naseem Faheem, a guard at St. Mark's Cathedral in Alexandria. On the day of the attack, he had stopped a man behaving suspiciously outside the cathedral. Seconds later, that man detonated a suicide bomb, killing Naseem and himself. Naseem, doing his job, saved dozens of lives. He was hailed as a hero—and a martyr.

On national television, just days after his death, his widow agreed to an interview. Surrounded by her children, she said something astonishing. "I'm not angry at the one who did this," she began. Then she addressed her husband's killer: "May God forgive you," and then she added, "and we also forgive you."

After that, the camera cut to the anchorman, Amr Adeeb, one of the most popular television personalities in Egypt—and a Muslim. Deeply moved, he struggled to find the words. Finally, he did. "The Christians of Egypt," he said, "are made of steel. How great is this forgiveness! This is their faith!"

This *is* our faith. Today's gospel reading challenges us: how great is *our* forgiveness? In the parable of the debtor, Jesus makes clear the judgment will be harsh "unless each of you forgives your brother from your heart." I'm reminded of Christ's own cry of forgiveness from the Cross. How great is our forgiveness?

ACT

How often do I forgive those who have hurt me? How often do I continue to hold a grudge? Today, I will give up something else for Lent: holding on to the past.

PRAY

Be merciful, O Lord, for I have sinned. Too often I have held a grudge or harbored an inability to forgive. Open my heart to let forgiveness take root and grow. Help me to forgive without end.

WEDNESDAY, MARCH 18
THIRD WEEK OF LENT

BEGIN

Lord, open my lips and my mouth shall proclaim your praise.

PRAY

Praise the LORD, Jerusalem.

~Psalm 147:12

LISTEN

Read Matthew 5:17–19.

"Do not think that I have come to abolish the law or the prophets. I have come not to abolish but to fulfill."

Fulfilling God's Plan

I remember chatting with a Benedictine monk several years ago while on retreat, and we talked about the challenges of living a life of poverty, chastity, and obedience. He spoke candidly about how prayer and commitment to the life made everything easier, along with an abiding love for the Lord. I asked him which of those three vows was the hardest. And without hesitation, he replied, "Obedience." Then he smiled and added, "That's the tough one, believe it or not."

It seems that even monks, like so many of us, don't like to be told what to do and aren't crazy about having to follow orders. No doubt that was also true in Jesus' day.

Obedience and following the Law were central to the life of Christ; he was, after all, an observant Jew.

But as this gospel makes clear, the commandments and the Law to him were only the beginning. This passage unfolds in the middle of his most famous address, the Sermon on the Mount, and after celebrating what makes someone blessed in the Beatitudes, he reminds his listeners that none of what he's saying is meant to contradict the Law. He is trying to build on it and fulfill it.

In some ways, isn't that what we are trying to do in Lent? By following the practices of this season—prayer, fasting, penance, almsgiving, and sacrifice—we strive to fulfill God's plan for us, his call to us, his invitation to grow in holiness and faith.

And isn't that worth the effort?

ACT

Do I struggle with obedience? Do I have a hard time with some of the practices and disciplines of Lent? Maybe I need to take it one day at a time. Just for today, I will work to live Lent with gratitude and joy, taking each moment as an opportunity to draw nearer to God.

PRAY

Be merciful, O Lord, for I have sinned. May the life of your Son serve to teach me how to be obedient, but through that obedience to grow in faith, hope, and charity. Amen.

THURSDAY, MARCH 19
SOLEMNITY OF ST. JOSEPH
THIRD WEEK OF LENT

BEGIN

Lord, open my lips and my mouth shall proclaim your praise.

PRAY

The promises of the LORD I will sing forever.

~*Psalm 89:2*

LISTEN

Read Matthew 1:16, 18–21.

"You are to name him Jesus, because he will save his people from their sins."

All We Need to Know

As we near the middle of Lent, the Church introduces a new figure into our journey, St. Joseph. Today marks the feast day of this great saint of steadfast silence. We know little about him from the scriptures, and there are no words attributed to him in the gospels. What does he have to teach us? Plenty.

In the 1980s, a minister named Robert Fulghum published a book called *All I Really Need to Know I Learned in Kindergarten*. A simple, straightforward guide to a humble, virtuous life, it stayed on the best-seller list for two years. Well, I'd suggest a lot of what we really need to know can be learned from St. Joseph.

Among other things, we learn from St. Joseph the following: Strive to be righteous. Stand by those you love, no matter what. Keep your commitments. Listen to angels. Don't worry so much about the future. Trust in God. Stay connected to your roots. Embrace the journey. Believe that God can be found anywhere, even when others don't make room for him. Dream. Dream again. And never stop dreaming.

And there is this: Don't be afraid to be quiet. Sometimes the silent partner has much to say. You can speak volumes just by being present, being strong, and being a model of obedient faith.

For those of us journeying through Lent, St. Joseph offers us companionship and inspiration; in Joseph, we find another person who journeyed, who made sacrifices, who made of his life a prayer, and who never lost sight of where God meant him to go. May he continue to travel with us and show us the way during these forty days.

ACT

We usually only see St. Joseph as a figure frozen in time—a statue, a holy card, a stained-glass window, or an icon. But he was a man like us, a father and husband and worker. How often do I jump to conclusions about others or turn them into stereotypes? Today, I will spend time appreciating the uniquely human dimensions of all those I meet and thanking God for his endless creativity.

PRAY

Be merciful, O Lord, for I have sinned. Guide me to be more like St. Joseph and become a more faithful follower of you. Amen.

Friday, March 20
Third Week of Lent

BEGIN

Lord, open my lips and my mouth shall proclaim your praise.

PRAY

Hear, my people, and I will admonish you; O Israel, will you not hear me?

~*Psalm 81*

LISTEN

Read Mark 12:28–34.

"Hear, O Israel! The Lord our God is Lord alone."

How Deep Is Your Love?

The Catholic writer and film critic Michael Lickona once said about marriage something I like to quote in my wedding homilies: "I believe," he wrote, "that marriage is the best chance I have to love my neighbor as myself." It's a great reminder that the person you will be spending your life with is going to be a very close neighbor—and that you should love that other person just as you love yourself.

In today's gospel reading, of course, loving your neighbor is one of the two great commandments. But we shouldn't forget, it is second to loving God. When we hear this reading, we tend to overlook the further instructions Jesus offers: that we are to love God "with all your heart, with all your soul, with all your mind, and with all your strength." It needs to be complete. You can't just phone it in.

Confronting this text during Lent poses a number of provocative questions. Are we holding anything back from God? Are we giving him everything we are—heart, soul, mind, and strength?

Ultimately, this brief passage invites us to explore the depths of our capacity to love—both loving God and loving our neighbor. We might also ask ourselves if we put forth the effort to love those around us who are, frankly, unlovable: the stubborn, the selfish, the hurtful, and the ones who have been broken by life. Do we see ourselves in them? Do we love them as we love ourselves?

A popular song from my youth asked, "How deep is your love?" It's a timeless question, really, and also a timely one for Lent.

ACT

Jesus tells us these are the most important laws to obey. So today, I will make it a priority to love God completely—with my heart, my soul, my mind, and my strength—and love my neighbor as much as myself.

PRAY

Be merciful, O Lord, for I have sinned. I have not always loved you or my neighbor as I should. Draw me closer to you, and deepen my faith and trust. Give me the courage and generosity of spirit to love those around me with the same patience and kindness that you love me. Amen.

Saturday, March 21
Third Week of Lent

BEGIN

Lord, open my lips and my mouth shall proclaim your praise.

PRAY

> Thoroughly wash me from my guilt and of my sin cleanse me.
>
> ~*Psalm 51:3–4*

LISTEN

> *Read Luke 18:9–14.*
>
> "Everyone who exalts himself will be humbled,
> and the one who humbles himself will be exalted."

A Little Lesson

A profound lesson in humility comes to us in the story of Jeanne Jugan. She was a French peasant woman, born in the late eighteenth century, who was deeply moved by the plight of the poor. In 1839, she founded the Little Sisters of the Poor, a religious order dedicated to care of the poor. That, in and of itself, was heroic. And so was what happened after.

Just a couple years after Jeanne founded the order, a priest was assigned to oversee it as chaplain. He decided to transfer Jeanne to another convent to train and work among the novices there. Out of obedience, she accepted the assignment and spent the rest of her life there. Many of the sisters who lived with her never knew that the sister who had so humbly lived and worked among them, this woman who emptied bedpans and swept floors, was the foundress of their order. It wasn't until an inquiry eleven years after her death that the truth came out. Jeanne Jugan never told anyone. She never demanded credit but accepted a life of relative obscurity out of love for the poor and desire to serve God.

As we continue our Lenten journey, and hear the parable of the exalted and the humble, we realize more deeply that humility is a part of holiness. The call of Lent is a call to humility, a call to realize our limitations and our weakness and make God a priority. The life of Jeanne Jugan is a stunning lesson of how the saints make it so.

What can we do to be more like them?

ACT

Just for today, I will humble myself before God, remembering that I began Lent marked with ashes as a sign of repentance and mortality. I will work to act out of love, not pride, giving the glory to God.

PRAY

Be merciful, O Lord, for I have sinned. This Lent, I remember that I am dust and to dust I will return. Help me, too, to return to the Gospel, living in simplicity and charity. Amen.

Laetare Sunday, March 22
Fourth Week of Lent

BEGIN

Lord, open my lips and my mouth shall proclaim your praise.

PRAY

> For you were once darkness, but now you are light in the Lord. Live as children of light.
>
> ~*Ephesians 5:8*

LISTEN

Read John 9:1–41.

"I am the light of the world."

Let In the Light

Looking for a break in the bleakness of Lent? Look no further. This Sunday, the light is here.

In the gospel reading, a blind man receives his sight, and Jesus makes this bold pronouncement: "I am the light of the world." When I think about what takes place in this passage, I think we witness here more than just a miracle. I see nothing less than another Genesis.

Remember the first words attributed to God at the very beginning of scripture:

"Let there be light." Light is where it all begins. This is how creation starts, how the universe is made, how the great and unending work of God's imagination takes off. And in this miracle, Jesus in his own way is repeating his Father's words: let there be light. Let creation begin. Let me help you see what you couldn't.

Jesus said that to a blind man two thousand years ago. And he says it to each of us today. *Let there be light.* Our gospel reading today cries out, *Let there be Christ, the light of the world. In him, we are given another Genesis.*

We began Lent being told to rend our hearts. Perhaps we need to do that to let in the light. Have we been selfish? Cruel? Merciless? Have we been too comfortable living in the shadows of cynicism and sin? Maybe we have been reluctant to love, closing off our hearts and allowing them to grow dark. Lent tells us, "Rend them. Tear them open. Let in the light."

ACT

Today, I will look for ways to bring more light into our dark and sometimes despairing world. Whom do I know who needs hope? Companionship? Encouragement? Prayer? Just for today, I welcome the light into my heart so I can reach out to others.

PRAY

Be merciful, O Lord, for I have sinned. Make me a channel of your peace and a bearer of your light. Amen.

MONDAY, MARCH 23
FOURTH WEEK OF LENT

BEGIN

Lord, open my lips and my mouth shall proclaim your praise.

PRAY

> Sing praise to the LORD, you his faithful ones, and
> give thanks to his holy name.
>
> ~*Psalm 30*

LISTEN

Read John 4:43–54.

"You may go, your son will live."

Believe

One of the most remarkable lines in today's gospel passage is so simple: "The man believed what Jesus said to him and left." What Jesus said, of course, was that his son would be cured. This is a stirring testament to belief. It's something we don't have nearly enough in our cynical age.

One person who believed was a priest named Fr. William McCarthy. Countless people in Quincy, Massachusetts, knew him simply as "Fr. Bill." In the late 1970s, he noticed the rise in homelessness in his neighborhood and wanted to do something about it. He set up cots in his church basement so that people could have someplace warm to spend the night. Eventually Fr. Bill found a building at the end of a dead-end street, next to the town's animal shelter, and there created "Fr. Bill's

Place," a sanctuary for people who had no place to go, no place they were wanted.

But Fr. Bill wanted them, and he wanted them to feel loved. When he died a few years ago, a former resident said, "He was everybody's priest." People remembered how they used to see Fr. Bill outside the building, sharing a cigarette with some of the residents—some sick, some alcoholic, others abandoned or abused. It was his flock. He fought for them and never gave up. And he did it because he believed. He believed in them. He believed in Jesus Christ. He believed in making miracles happen. And because of his belief, they, too, believed.

Lent encourages us to nurture our belief and trust that God can work miracles in us and through us. He can. He will. If only, like the royal official in today's gospel and like Fr. Bill McCarthy, we take his word for it.

ACT

Today, I will set aside doubt. I will choose to believe that God can work miracles in my life, and I will believe in the possibility of miracles in the lives of others too.

PRAY

Be merciful, O Lord, for I have sinned. Help my unbelief, and help me to trust more deeply in your love for me.

Tuesday, March 24
Fourth Week of Lent

BEGIN

Lord, open my lips and my mouth shall proclaim your praise.

PRAY

God is our refuge and our strength.

~Psalm 46:2

LISTEN

Read John 5:1–16.

"Rise, take up your mat and walk."

The Rising

Who could possibly say no to Jesus?

In today's gospel reading, Jesus encounters a man crippled for most of his life and asks him one question, "Do you want to be well?" But the man doesn't answer yes. Instead, he explains why he has been unable to go to the healing waters—other people kept getting in the way! So Jesus, in effect, brings the healing waters to him, with one simple command. "Rise," Jesus tells him, "take up your mat and walk." And so he does.

It's probably one of the briefest and most perfunctory miracles in the gospels, but it is packed with significance for all of us. Lent reminds us that all of us, in one way or another, are cripples. We are human. We are stubbornly, painfully imperfect. We may be crippled by fear, insecurity, or sin; we may be crippled by bad habits or pettiness or ego or greed. But we want to get to another place. We want to move on. Perhaps others get in the way. Maybe we find ourselves frustrated by our weaknesses. But Jesus offers this moment of redemption and hope: if we want to be well, he can help make it so. He brings us his healing word.

This season is a time for listening to Christ's call. Do we want to be well? Do we want to rise, take up our mat, and walk? Whatever may be holding us back, whatever may be crippling us, Christ offers his word of encouragement and healing. Do we want to be well? Who could say no?

ACT

Just for today, I will have the courage to let go of whatever is crippling me, whatever is inhibiting me, and whatever is holding me back from a deeper relationship with the Lord.

PRAY

Be merciful, O Lord, for I have sinned. I yearn to grow in holiness and get past my sins, my weaknesses, and my faults. Give me the grace to do what I need to do. Amen.

Wednesday, March 25

Feast of the Annunciation
Fourth Week of Lent

BEGIN

Lord, open my lips and my mouth shall proclaim your praise.

PRAY

> Here I am, Lord, I come to do your will.
>
> ~*Psalm 40:9*

LISTEN

Read Luke 1:26–38.

"Hail, favored one, the Lord is with you!"

How Can This Be?

Once again, we find a surprising visitor joining us during Lent: the angel Gabriel, bringing some news to Mary that will upend her world and change history. Life is like that.

How many of us have been blindsided by events we never expected—a twist on life's path that we never saw coming, for better or for worse—and asked ourselves, in fury or despair or bewilderment, How can this be?

And here Mary is told only, "Nothing is impossible with God." And that is enough. That is all she needs to hear. She will accept God's will, and she will carry it out. It is—in every sense—extraordinary. How is it that someone so young so easily said yes to what would undoubtedly be difficult, painful, and maybe even scandalous? The very idea of it is a shock. It goes against our culture.

We live at a time when it's so easy to say no. We can make life what we want it to be, even if that's not what it *should* be. But Mary listened to another voice, the voice of an angel with an invitation from God. When Mary asked the question the world asks so often of God—"How can this be?"—the answer ignited in her a fire. The fire of the Holy Spirit, the fire of possibility. Because nothing is impossible with God. How often we forget that! How often we disbelieve it, or mistrust it.

During these last days of Lent, as we continue working to recommit ourselves to the Lord, consider this another kind of annunciation—announcing encouragement, promising hope, and inviting us to be excited by possibility. Because, of course, God can make anything possible.

ACT

Today, like Mary, I will put myself in God's hands, trusting that he will take me where he wants me to go because nothing is impossible with God.

PRAY

Be merciful, O Lord, for I have sinned. How often I haven't trusted you! How often I've questioned you or doubted! Reassure my skeptical heart, and strengthen it to do your will for me. Amen.

Thursday, March 26
Fourth Week of Lent

Lord, open my lips and my mouth shall proclaim your praise.

PRAY

> Remember us, Lord, as you favor your people.
>
> ~*Psalm 106:4*

LISTEN

> *Read John 5:31–47.*
>
> "I have testimony greater than John's."

Giving Testimony

This brief passage from John's gospel gives us one word again and again: *testimony. Testimony* or *testify* appear no less than eight times in just a few lines. *Webster's* tells us that *testimony* means "a solemn declaration usually made orally by a witness under oath in response to interrogation by a lawyer or authorized public official." But it is also "the tablets inscribed with the Mosaic Law" and "a divine decree attested in the scriptures." However one interprets it, what is happening in this passage is something of great import; Jesus clearly means it is not something to be taken lightly.

Among other things, he reminds his listeners that what he is teaching and doing, the miracles he is performing and the lessons he is imparting, go further and deeper than his followers may realize. He is proclaiming a "solemn declaration" that comes, in fact, from the

Father—a message of transformation and conversion, a promise of salvation.

In this, Jesus testifies, makes a solemn oath, to mercy. He testifies to charity. He testifies to compassion and sacrifice, to prayer and penance. He testifies to love. In many ways, he is testifying to the practices we are seeking to live this Lent and assuring us that what he is teaching us to do and believe comes from above.

And he is asking us to give testimony as well. We do it daily with our choices, our words, and our prayers— and most importantly, with our lives. This season, again and again we are hearing Christ's testimony.

What are people hearing in ours?

ACT

If we were called to testify on behalf of the Gospel, what would we say? This day, I will pray for the courage to live out my faith selflessly and joyfully.

PRAY

Be merciful, O Lord, for I have sinned. Make me more courageous, more loving, more compassionate, and more prayerful so I can give testimony to your presence in my life. Amen.

Friday, March 27
Fourth Week of Lent

BEGIN

Lord, open my lips and my mouth shall proclaim your praise.

PRAY

The LORD is close to the brokenhearted.

~Psalm 34:19

LISTEN

Read John 7:1–2, 10, 25–30.

Some of the inhabitants of Jerusalem said,
"Is he not the one they are trying to kill?"

We Know Him

We're getting closer to the end of the Lent now; Good Friday is only two weeks away, and the readings are taking a more somber tone. There is a mood of foreboding in this gospel passage and a sense that the end is near. Jesus is speaking directly to those who question, who search, and who doubt. "You know me," he tells them, "and also know where I am from."

Is he speaking to us? Are we still having trouble finding our way as these forty days near an end? These final days of Lent can challenge us just as Jesus challenges his listeners. We may feel frustrated, confused, and inadequate. We may feel burdened by fasting or praying. We may be waiting for an epiphany of sorts, an "Aha!" moment that makes all the Lenten effort and discipline click into place.

Maybe we're being tempted by the Easter chocolate on display in the stores, or pausing to gaze longingly at the posters of Happy Meals hanging in the neighborhood McDonald's. We might even be bored; is it Easter yet?

Jesus' words can snap us back to reality: "You know me."

Yes, of course. We do. We have spent these weeks listening to his words, reliving his miracles, and following his own journey toward Calvary, and we've been following him with our prayers, our hopes, and our moments of sacrifice and soul-searching. We know him. And he knows us. These last two weeks can be a time for even deeper reflection and recommitment to our own conversion, and a reminder that we are not making this journey on our own. We are walking with Christ, as he walks with us.

We know him: his teachings, his expectations, his mercy, and his love. And we know, too, why we are doing all this and where this journey leads.

ACT

I will spend time today reflecting on where my Lenten journey has taken me—and where I still hope to go. And I will trust that Jesus will be there, as he always has been, as my hope, as my brother, and as my guide.

PRAY

Be merciful, O Lord, for I have sinned. May I spend these last days of Lent recommitting myself to you, trusting in your love, and witnessing to your mercy and compassion. Amen.

Saturday, March 28

Fourth Week of Lent

BEGIN

Lord, open my lips and my mouth shall proclaim your praise.

PRAY

O Lord, my God, in you I take refuge.

~Psalm 7:2

LISTEN

Read John 7:40–53.

Some in the crowd who heard these words said, "This is truly the Prophet."

The Divided Flock

On March 21, 2006, a social media pioneer named Jack Dorsey did something no one had ever done before, and it had a profound impact on all of us. He sent out the first tweet. "Just setting up my twttr," he wrote. The rest is history (and Twitter soon added vowels to its name).

At last report, there are about five hundred million tweets per day sent from around the world, with some hundred million daily active Twitter users. And the numbers keep growing. We live, of course, in an age when communication is instantaneous, when no thought goes unexpressed, and when more voices are being heard by more people—for better or worse. And a lot of it is happening on Twitter and other forms of social media.

It's also sparking a lot of vitriol and outright anger. But this gospel reminds us that's hardly new. Humans can't help but disagree. Indeed, it sounds as if everybody had an opinion about Jesus—not all favorable. Many of those who heard him then were as divided as those who frequent Facebook today. Some were awestruck; others, angry. This might make us ask ourselves, What is our opinion of Jesus? How do *we* see him? How has that affected us during Lent?

In a world where everybody has an opinion of Jesus—again, not all favorable—we remember that day a few weeks ago when we wore ashes and showed who we are, and whom we follow. We remember our commitment to turn our hearts back to the Lord.

And we remember, too, that we are people guided by love to live differently than those who value other things first. That's a message with far greater impact than anything Jack Dorsey could have imagined.

ACT

How can I send the message today that I am a follower of Christ? The best way is with my life, so I will strive to live as a faith-filled Christian, witnessing to the Gospel with compassion and joy.

PRAY

Be merciful, O Lord, for I have sinned. Make me unafraid to proclaim my faith in you with my life—loving boldly, forgiving generously, and enduring patiently whatever trials I face. Amen.

Sunday, March 29
Fifth Sunday of Lent

BEGIN

Lord, open my lips and my mouth shall proclaim your praise.

PRAY

If Christ is in you, although the body is dead because of sin, the spirit is alive because of righteousness.

~Romans 8:10

LISTEN

Read John 11:1–45.

"This illness is not to end in death, but is for the glory of God, that the Son of God may be glorified through it."

Leaving the Tomb

For many years one of the most influential priests in America was someone most have never heard of: Fr. Joseph Martin.

Over many years he gave talks around the country. The most powerful talks all began with the same seven words: "I'm Joe Martin, and I'm an alcoholic." Two of Fr. Martin's talks—called "chalk talks," because he used a blackboard—were filmed and became standard viewing at treatment centers and hospitals all over the United States. He helped countless people he had never even met. One doctor said of him, "Fr. Martin has done more to help those suffering from addiction than anyone in the last fifty years."

Fr. Martin often spoke candidly of his own struggle with alcoholism: times when he was afraid to go near the altar because of his drinking, Sundays when his hands trembled, and the time he was confined to a psychiatric ward. He was eventually sent to Guest House, a treatment center for clergy, where he turned his life around and began the slow process of turning around the lives of tens of thousands of others.

A few months before he died, Fr. Martin marked fifty years of sobriety. And he spoke of his journey in terms that can resonate with each of us, as we reflect on today's gospel story of Lazarus and look forward to the bright hope of Easter. "How can I explain," he asked, "what it feels like to be risen from the tomb of addiction?"

Lent is a time when we answer Christ's call and come out of whatever personal tomb might be confining us, the sins and setbacks framing our lives. Lent asks us to rise and walk away from them. Like Lazarus, Fr. Martin knew what it was to answer the call to "come out." May we find the courage this season to do the same.

ACT

Do I feel sometimes as if I am living in my own personal tomb of brokenness? Jesus is calling all of us to come out into the light. I will commit myself to answering his call this day, and every day, and seek to begin a new life in his grace.

PRAY

Be merciful, O Lord, for I have sinned. Lead me to the light of your face, the light of your hope, and the light of a new life with you. Amen.

MONDAY, MARCH 30
FIFTH WEEK OF LENT

BEGIN

Lord, open my lips and my mouth shall proclaim your praise.

PRAY

The LORD is my shepherd, I shall not want.

~Psalm 23:1

LISTEN

Read John 8:1–11.

"Where are they? Has no one condemned you?"

Seeing the Light

Near the end of his life, the novelist William Styron took a courageous step and described his battle with depression in a book, *Darkness Visible*. Depression is a medical condition affecting millions of us, but many people don't want to talk about it, or aren't sure quite how to do that. A famous, successful figure, Styron came forward and wrote about how depression had touched his life. He described the despair he experienced, the sense of helplessness, and how the medical treatment he received helped to bring him back, at last, to the light. At one point, he quoted from Dante's *Inferno*: "In the middle of the journey of our life I found myself in a dark wood / For I had lost the right path."

In so many ways, that describes the journey of all of us, struggling to find our way in a world of confusion and chaos. It might also describe the journey of this anonymous woman in today's gospel passage—caught in adultery, humiliated, and possibly confronting the last moments of her life. But along comes Jesus. Everything changes. And she is able to begin anew. In fact, this encounter reassures us that change is possible, that healing can happen, and that forgiveness is within our grasp. It's a beautiful illustration of Lent's deepest meaning: that the bleakness of this present time will be broken at Easter and light will again shine. God will bring forth new life.

The last words of Styron's book continue the same quotation from Dante, giving us words that proclaim a beautiful and enduring truth, and the heart-stopping hope we hold onto:

"And so we came forth," Dante wrote, "and once again beheld the stars."

ACT

We need to remember that Lent is a time of healing and hope, and that God's mercy awaits us. Today, I will be grateful for the gift of this season and this period of reflection and renewal.

PRAY

Be merciful, O Lord, for I have sinned. Thank you, Lord, for your mercy, your compassion, and your extended hand of friendship that reminds me I can always begin again and that every day offers me another opportunity to grow in faith and holiness. Amen.

Tuesday, March 31
Fifth Week of Lent

BEGIN

Lord, open my lips and my mouth shall proclaim your praise.

PRAY

O LORD, hear my prayer and let my cry come to you.

~*Psalm 102:2*

LISTEN

Read John 8:21–30.

"The one who sent me is with me."

The God Who Is There

In the late sixties and early seventies, the president of *CBS News* was a colorful and very gifted man by the name of Richard Salant. By the time I'd arrived at CBS in the early eighties, he was long gone, but his leadership was legendary. And someone once shared with me a favorite Salant quotation. "There are only two kinds of people in the world," he said. "Those who are there when I need them, and those who aren't."

Hearing this gospel passage, I can't help but think Jesus was the former. During his earthly life, he was there when his Father needed him—even unto death. He and the Father were inseparable. "The one who sent me is with me," Jesus tells his listeners. "He has not left me alone, because I always do what is pleasing to him." One of the challenges of Lent is to try to follow Christ's perfect example and "do what is pleasing" to God. We spend these weeks examining our lives, inspecting our faults, and picking apart our choices. We may fall prey to going too far, being too scrupulous. Are we doing enough? Are we doing too much?

Prayer can uplift us and comfort us. So can remembering something Jesus underscores in today's gospel: "He has not left me alone." When we seek to please God, he is with us. He will not leave us alone. Throughout these days of Lent, the Father has opened his arms to us, welcoming us, encouraging us, and comforting us when we feel we've fallen short. Whether we realize it or not, he's the one who is always there when we need him.

ACT

Have I forgotten God's role in my life? His closeness to me? This day, I will try to be more aware of his presence and seek it in my life, my work, and in all whom I meet.

PRAY

Be merciful, O Lord, for I have sinned. Help me to remember your nearness to me, even when I feel I've fallen away from you. May I always feel your presence close to my heart. Amen.

WEDNESDAY, APRIL 1
FIFTH WEEK OF LENT

BEGIN

Lord, open my lips and my mouth shall proclaim your praise.

PRAY

The LORD is gracious and merciful.

~Psalm 145:8

LISTEN

Read John 8:31–42.

"If you remain in my word, you will truly be my disciples."

Free to Be

In the spring of 2007, the British journalist Alan Johnston of the BBC was kidnapped in Gaza by a group known as the Palestinian Army of Islam. The story caused a sensation around the world. There were protests and appeals on his behalf, a worldwide outcry from the journalism community, and petitions circulated appealing for his release. Finally, after weeks of uncertainty, and even reports of his execution, he was freed. He had been captive for 114 days. Facing the press for the first time, he struggled to put his experience into words. "It was really grim," he said, "an appalling experience. It was like being buried alive. Countless times I dreamed of being free."

"Being free," of course, is one of the themes in the gospel reading today. If you know the truth, Jesus tells his followers, you will be free. At the time, people thought he was talking about slavery and human bondage. But here and now, we know he is speaking about our very human slavery to sin, shackles that can keep us from living in the light of Christ. If we understand why those chains are holding us and confining us—and if we can embrace the truth of Christ's message of faith, hope, and love—we can be free.

These last days of Lent turn our eyes more and more to the wood of the Cross; Jesus speaks repeatedly of his impending death. But what about the chains of sin that bind us? Let us listen anew to his message, using this time to pray, to resolve, to repent—and to step from those shackles in order to be free.

ACT

What chains are holding me back? What walls are keeping me from God? What truth am I avoiding? Today, I will undertake a closer examination of my life and my choices and have the courage to be honest with myself. I'll take a big step toward personal and spiritual freedom in Christ.

PRAY

Be merciful, O Lord, for I have sinned. You know better than I do what is holding me back. Open my eyes and open my heart to be fully free in your love. Amen.

THURSDAY, APRIL 2
FIFTH WEEK OF LENT

BEGIN

Lord, open my lips and my mouth shall proclaim your praise.

PRAY

> Look to the LORD in his strength; seek to serve him constantly.
>
> ~*Psalm 105:4*

LISTEN

Read John 8:51–59.

"Whoever keeps my word will never see death."

Keeping His Word

This section of scripture begins with an allusion to never seeing death—and then concludes with Jesus fleeing to *avoid* death. (In a striking irony, Christ's accusers pick up stones, just as they had done earlier in this chapter with the adulterous woman.)

Throughout this section, we hear a lot of questions, debate, accusations, and outright skepticism. But the words of Jesus in the opening sentence of today's gospel reading stick with me: "Whoever keeps my word will never see death." Isn't this what we are striving for, working for, praying for, and sacrificing for? Isn't this key to our understanding of Lent? Oh, we know we will die—Ash Wednesday reminded us of that, vividly—and we know we have work to do with whatever time we have on this earth. The salvation of our souls is at stake, which is precisely why we need to pay special heed just now to those cautionary words of Jesus.

We aren't trying to skip the grave; we are working to have eternal life. And to do that we need to keep Christ's word—and hold it close in our hearts. John's gospel is where we hear most explicitly and directly what that word is: "Love one another as I have loved you." That passage is so familiar, we might almost consider that phrase a cliché. But when we consider what it portends—love beyond all measure, love even to the point of death—we cannot help but be brought up short, because we realize how often *we* come up short.

Let us redouble our efforts to truly keep Christ's word this Lent, realizing anew that it alone can give us new life.

ACT

Just for today, I will keep my heart attuned to the word of God and remember that keeping that word can lead me to eternal life.

PRAY

Be merciful, O Lord, for I have sinned. Too often I have neglected your word or taken it for granted. May I hear it with not only my ears but also my heart.

Friday, April 3

Fifth Week of Lent

BEGIN

Lord, open my lips and my mouth shall proclaim your praise.

PRAY

> I love you, O Lord, my strength, O Lord my rock, my fortress, my deliverer.
>
> ~*Psalm 18:2–3*

LISTEN

Read John 10:31–42.

"The Father is in me and I am in the Father."

Living in Him

Probably the last place you would expect to find a lesson in Christology is in *The Lion King*, but there it is, halfway through the second act of the popular stage production, when the cast sings the triumphal anthem "He Lives in You." Of course, they're singing about African heritage, and the legacy of the deceased lion king being passed on to his young son, Simba. But every time I hear it (I confess, the Broadway cast album is on my iPhone), I am reminded of this exchange in John's gospel. I don't know if the creators of *The Lion King* did this consciously (I'm guessing, probably not), but it resonates in every believing Christian's heart.

The Father lives on in the Son—and, by extension, in us. What does this mean for us on our Lenten journey? I think it helps us realize the vital importance of God's presence in our lives, spiritually and sacramentally. He lives in us through how *we* live—and how we love. And we receive added graces when we receive him in the Eucharist and bind ourselves to him through the Sacrament of Reconciliation.

Considered that way, how could we not want to draw closer to him during Lent? How could we not want to amend our lives and convert our hearts? How could we not want to avoid the heartbreak of sin and rejoice in the one who lives in us?

ACT

This day, I will remind myself that God lives in Christ and wants to live fully in me. I will work to make that happen, with renewed fervor and joy!

PRAY

Be merciful, O Lord, for I have sinned. My deepest prayer is to let you live more fully in me. Help me to make that so during Lent and always.

Saturday, April 4

Fifth Week of Lent

BEGIN

Lord, open my lips and my mouth shall proclaim your praise.

PRAY

"I will be their God and they shall be my people."

~*Ezekiel 37:27*

LISTEN

Read John 11:45–56.

Now many of the Jews who had come to Mary and seen what he had done began to believe in him.

Fear Factor

In the gospel today, the talk among the Jewish leaders grows more heated about the need to do something about Jesus, and the discussion takes on a more urgent tone as well.

What strikes me about this exchange is that the Pharisees respond, first and foremost, from a place of fear. They are terrified of losing land and power. "If we leave him alone," one of them says, "all will believe in him, and the Romans will come and take away both our land and our nation." We can't help but feel a certain empathy. How often have we faced a similar crisis and feared for our own well-being? How often do we find ourselves uncertain about what to do or how to handle a crisis out of fear that we will do something wrong?

This moment in the gospel has a discomforting familiarity. But it also challenges us to consider what we would have done in similar circumstances. Would we have been any more courageous?

Lent asks us to do just that: to be people of courage. These weeks have asked us to examine ourselves fearlessly. We have tried to pray more deeply, sacrifice more humbly, extend ourselves more generously, and embrace more completely our call as followers of Christ. It hasn't always been easy. And sometimes, it can be unsettling, even frightening. But there is something greater calling us forward too. In these last days, we need to remind ourselves why we are doing what we are doing—and wait in joyful hope for the bright promise of Easter.

ACT

Have I found myself during Lent feeling insecure or fearful? Have I held myself back from self-examination because I was afraid of what I might find out about myself? Today, I will let down my guard and consider what Christ gave for me, and I will give myself fully to these last days of prayer, almsgiving, and fasting.

PRAY

Be merciful, O Lord, for I have sinned. Guide me to love you more fully, more fearlessly. Give me courage to stand up for what I believe in and to give myself to you with a generous and joyful heart.

SUNDAY, APRIL 5

PALM SUNDAY

BEGIN

Lord, open my lips and my mouth shall proclaim your praise.

PRAY

> They divide my garments among them, and for my vesture they cast lots. But you, O LORD, be not far from me.
>
> ~*Psalm 22:19–20*

LISTEN

Read Matthew 21:9.

> The crowds preceding him and those following kept crying out and saying: "Hosanna to the Son of David; blessed is he who comes in the name of the Lord; hosanna in the highest."

Our Fate in Our Hands

Is there anything more Catholic than the palms we receive this Sunday? We save them, display them, and tuck them behind mirrors or holy pictures. These palms tell part of the story we hear at Mass this Sunday, the Passion. But they also tell *our* story.

Five weeks ago, we received ashes to remind us of our mortality, our sinfulness, and our need for conversion. Those ashes were the remnants of burned palms. This Sunday, here we are, five weeks older. Hopefully, five weeks wiser. And we hold in our hands new palms—new growth. And this prompts the question, How have we grown since that Wednesday in February?

How have we changed? And what will we do with the promise, the potential, we now hold in our hands?

Our hope is that we have been renewed during these weeks. And just maybe, these palms can remind us of that. They remind us of Christ's suffering and death, the triumph of that ride into Jerusalem, and the tragedy of Calvary. They remind us of our role in that passion, that what Christ suffered, he suffered for us. And they remind us of how this Lenten journey began, marked with ashes that once were palms.

The ashes we received five weeks ago were washed away. But these palms stay with us, offering silent testimony and nudging us to remember that we, too, will one day be dust. My prayer this Palm Sunday is that we carry that memory with us, just as we carry these palms. Each of us holds our future in our hands this day. What will we do with it?

ACT

This Palm Sunday, I will do more than just use the palms as a holy decoration. I will consider what they really mean. What more can I do to give myself more completely to God and grow in my faith?

PRAY

Be merciful, O Lord, for I have sinned. Give me grace to see in the palms I hold the promise of a new beginning, a new growth in holiness as I draw to a close this season of prayer and penance. Fill me with new life. Amen.

MONDAY, APRIL 6
HOLY WEEK

BEGIN

Lord, open my lips and my mouth shall proclaim your praise.

PRAY

> I believe that I shall see the bounty of the LORD
> in the land of the living.
>
> *~Psalm 27:13*

LISTEN

> *Read John 12:1–11.*
>
> "You always have the poor with you, but you do not always have me."

Remembering the Poor

Mother Teresa used to tell people she met that they should always be aware that they carry the Gospel in their hands. And she would reach out and touch each finger on the stranger's hand and say, quoting scripture, "You did this for me." Whatever you did for the least of these, she would remind them, you did for me. Never forget that, she said. Use your hands to live the Gospel.

Caring for the poor is one of the cornerstones of our Lenten practices, giving alms, dedicating time to charity, and remembering "the least of these." And in this gospel passage from John, it falls to Judas to ask if money spent on fine oil should rather go to the poor. "You always have the poor with you, but you do not always have me," Jesus responds pointedly, signaling that his time on earth is drawing to a close. But as Mother Teresa knew, honoring the poor honors Christ. We show our love for him in our love for others, especially the most vulnerable, the desperate, and the outcast. If we have neglected them this Lent, we have also neglected Jesus. We have overlooked one of the most fundamental aspects of the Christian life, concern for the poor.

Jesus suffered, died, and rose for us, but every day we are reminded that his suffering goes on among the neediest of our brothers and sisters. They are always with us, Jesus said. And we carry an important reminder of that in our hands. How will we use them?

ACT

Have I neglected the poor this Lent? Have I remembered to see the face of Christ in the faces of the poor? Today, I will search my conscience to see if I have given enough of my time and treasure to remember those so often forgotten.

PRAY

Be merciful, O Lord, for I have sinned. Make my heart more generous, more compassionate, and more able to give to those in need and to know you in them. Amen.

TUESDAY, APRIL 7
HOLY WEEK

BEGIN

Lord, open my lips and my mouth shall proclaim your praise.

PRAY

> In you, O LORD, I take refuge; let me never be put to shame.
>
> *~Psalm 71:1*

LISTEN

Read John 13:21–33, 36–38.

"My children, I will be with you only a little while longer."

Being There

Can you imagine what it must have been like? To be in that room, at that meal, that last supper? To hear that conversation, to see the exchange of glances around the table, and to taste the bread and wine being shared? Then there's a noise, as one of the Twelve gets up suddenly to leave. Which one? Oh, Judas. What could he possibly be doing? Where could he be going at this time of night? The Gospel of John paints a scene of confusion and uncertainty. The Messiah sits among them, but no one quite realizes what is happening—or what is about to happen. There's a sense of distractedness. No one imagines that history is about to change and that, in a matter of hours, nothing will ever be the same.

It is like that so often in our own lives, isn't it? Maybe we have experienced that during Lent too: a sense of disengagement, disinterest, frustration, distraction, or temptation. It can be hard to keep our thoughts and our hearts focused on prayer, to remember to fast, and to stay focused on the "reason for the season," which is our own interior conversion.

But as Lent nears its end and we begin to take stock of where we are, and where we have been, take a moment to reflect on where it began. Use these last days to put yourself in that room with the apostles. Imagine what it must have been like. And remember that we know today what they didn't know then: that the Resurrection was about to happen. That, ultimately, is the greatest reason for this season, and the greatest reason to be humbled and grateful for the journey we are taking.

ACT

If I have found myself distracted or sometimes indifferent to Lent, today that changes. This day, I will whisper a prayer of gratitude for this time of reflection and renewal and consider what I have gained.

PRAY

Be merciful, O Lord, for I have sinned. God, in your mercy, grant me the grace to appreciate where this Lenten journey has taken me, and help me follow where you lead. Amen.

Wednesday, April 8
Holy Week

BEGIN

Lord, open my lips and my mouth shall proclaim your praise.

PRAY

> LORD, in your great love, answer me.
>
> *~Psalm 69:14*

LISTEN

Read Matthew 26:14–25.

"Amen, I say to you, one of you will betray me."

Beyond Betrayal

Traditionally, this day is known as "Spy Wednesday," when Judas spent his time spying for an opportunity to betray Jesus and turn him over to the authorities. His turning against Jesus was so grave, and his act so devastating, that the name of Judas become synonymous with betrayal. The name *Judas* has even worked its way into gardening and horticulture. There is a colorful plant known as the "Judas tree," the tree some think was used by Judas to take his life. This beautiful tree, native to the Mediterranean, bears brilliant deep pink flowers in the spring, flowers that legend tells us are said to have blushed in shame after Judas's death.

Betrayal comes in many sizes and shapes. Maybe this day is a moment for us to pause and reflect on the ways we have turned against the Lord, to examine our consciences and our hearts. Have we ever been, in effect, a Judas to Christ? Have we betrayed the Gospel—turned against Christ's command to love? Have we felt shame, sorrow, or disappointment in ourselves?

Lent is our opportunity to make amends. It is our opportunity to help make right what we have done wrong, to redirect our thoughts, refocus our prayers, and convert our hearts. How can we take what we have learned these days and make a difference in the days and weeks to come?

If we have lived with sorrow for our sins, if we have somehow turned against Christ, we don't have to live in eternal shame; we don't need to be like the Judas tree. The promise of the Resurrection, the very promise we will celebrate this coming Sunday, tells us we can know another way.

ACT

Today, I will examine my choices and redouble my efforts to be a faithful disciple of Jesus.

PRAY

Be merciful, O Lord, for I have sinned. Deepen my dedication to you, uplift my heart, and make me a more faithful follower of your word. Amen.

Thursday, April 9
Holy Thursday

BEGIN

Lord, open my lips and my mouth shall proclaim your praise.

PRAY

> How shall I make a return to the LORD for all the good he has done for me?

~*Psalm 116:12*

LISTEN

Read John 13:1–15.

"I have given you a model to follow, so that as I have done for you, you should also do."

God on His Knees

A few years ago, the History Channel showed a documentary in which scientists studying the Shroud of Turin used computer technology and clues and markings from the shroud to create a 3-D image of the face of Christ. The result is a realistic portrait of a young man with long hair, a beard, scars, and blood stains around his brow. He looks heavier, more muscular than most may think.

But if you want yet another image of Jesus, look to the gospel reading for Holy Thursday. This picture may be even more surprising. We see him on his knees, washing feet. For all those who ask the perennial question "What would Jesus do?" here is your answer. *This* is truly what it means to be Christ. "I have given you a model to follow," he says. "As I have done for you, you should also do."

This day, God gets down on his knees for us. He becomes a servant—as humble as a slave, as meager and plain as a crumb of bread. Here is where we learn what it means to be like Christ. As we enter the final hours of Holy Week, it's a good time to ask ourselves how we have lived that model during Lent. Have we served? Have we sacrificed? Have we bent down to help others?

The fact remains: if you want to really know what Jesus looked like, you won't find it on the History Channel. Look instead to this day's gospel. Here—on his knees before others, his head lowered in humility and in love—*here* is where you see the truest image of Christ.

ACT

How can I more completely model Jesus' humility? What can I do to serve others? Today, I will spend time prayerfully remembering Christ's love for all of us, and I will try to live as he taught me, not just during these last hours of Lent but every day.

PRAY

Be merciful, O Lord, for I have sinned. Give me a clean heart, to love you more fully. Help me to remember the power of your mercy, the tenderness of your love, and the fullness of your sacrifice for me. Amen.

Greg Kandra serves as a deacon in the Diocese of Brooklyn and is a multimedia editor at the Catholic Near East Welfare Association. He is the author of *Daily Devotions for Advent 2018* and writes *The Deacon's Bench* blog. Kandra was a writer and producer for CBS News from 1982 to 2008 for programs including *The CBS Evening News with Katie Couric*, *Sunday Morning*, *60 Minutes II*, and *48 Hours*. He also served for four years as a writer and producer on the live finale of the hit reality show *Survivor*.

Kandra has received two Peabody and two Emmy awards, four Writers Guild of America awards, three Catholic Press Association awards, and a Christopher Award for his work. He also was named 2017 Clergy of the Year by the Catholic Guild of Our Lady of the Skies Chapel at JFK International Airport. He earned a bachelor's degree in English from the University of Maryland. Kandra cowrote the acclaimed CBS documentary *9/11*. He contributed to three books, including Dan Rather's *Deadlines and Datelines*, and a homily series. His work has been published in *America*, *US Catholic*, *Busted Halo*, and *The Brooklyn Tablet*. He has been a regular guest on Catholic radio.

Kandra lives with his wife, Siobhain, in the New York City area.

patheos.com/blogs/deaconsbench/
Facebook: @TheDeaconsBench
Twitter: @DeaconGregK

AVE
AVE MARIA PRESS

Founded in 1865, Ave Maria Press,
a ministry of the Congregation of
Holy Cross, is a Catholic publishing
company that serves the spiritual and
formative needs of the Church and its
schools, institutions, and ministers;
Christian individuals and families; and
others seeking spiritual nourishment.

For a complete listing of titles from

Ave Maria Press

Sorin Books

Forest of Peace

Christian Classics

visit www.avemariapress.com

AVE MARIA PRESS
Notre Dame, IN
A Ministry of the United States Province of Holy Cross